Started reading
July 8 2018

METATRON

This is the Clarion Call!

Greetings, welcome, I am Lord Metatron – the Angelic presence that encompasses the Universe. We are here to help you move forward in your Spiritual development and with everything that is happening on the Earth plane at the moment. Your material existence, as you understand it, is changing and everything is changing on your Planet for the better. It may seem as if it is not changing for the better for there are disasters, there are floods, Earthquakes, financial difficulties. There is Famine, Greed, corruption and negativity on the Earth plane. And there are Power Players that are there who seem to be controlling everything. Your Conspiracy theories are not without foundation. However you must understand that although there is an organisation that is happening of the Earth Plane. Ultimately you will move forward towards freedom and not slavery. Therefore accept what is moving forward for yourselves and concentrate individually on your own vessel, on your own being, on your own spirituality. To do this is to do your part for Ascension. Ascension is the change of consciousness that you are all going through. From the lowest to the highest as far as you see it where your spirituality is concerned. Everyone is feeling the change, feeling a difference. Not everyone can understand it, not everybody can pinpoint it. But everybody is feeling it on the Earth plane. You must relax, you must Love, for Love is the key to your transformation. You are multidimensional beings and you have the potential to create Worlds, to create Universes, to create other Big Bangs. At the beginning of the creation of this Universe, yes, there was a physical big bang. Do you think there was nothing before creation, before the Big Bang. (Laughs) Love has always been here and there are many Universes happening simultaneously right now. That are being created, that are imploding, that are moving forward. Your Universe is just at the beginning. Although in your linear time it seems like a long time for it is millions and billions of years. It is merely a sniff in the understanding of time as far as Spirit, the Angels and your understanding of God is concerned. You must come to an acceptance of the concept that you are creator beings. You are creating this reality, you are moving this forward. This is a wonderful thing to comprehend for you are only now becoming conscious of your own consciousness - which is going to take this Planet to the next stage of your Evolution. This is a conscious spiritual Evolution and a technological evolution. All different areas must be moved forward. But now and for the next fifty years the concentration will be on your population becoming more spiritual and in becoming more spiritual it will be related and translated to a practical level where all the beings on your Earth are fed, watered, clothed, comforted and made to feel as one. You are coming together. There are still obstacles to overcome, of course, but you are going to move forward and transform. We have great hope for the World. We have great Love for the World. And we are nurturing each and every one of you. Though you are in a diverse, leading edge creative experiment of consciousness. You must accept yourselves for this understanding that you are creating your own reality. There are certain things that are going to happen. That are meant to happen and that will always happen. If you understand the concept of an Acorn growing into a mighty Oak tree, you will understand that the Acorn always has the potential to grow into an Oak tree. And it will always grow into an Oak tree when it is planted and given the right nurturance from Mother Nature, the Earth. It will never grow into a Cherry bush. Therefore understand your design. As humans you are here as conscious Spiritual Beings. And it is your destiny, or your design, whichever way you can understand this concept. This is where you are heading. To hold yourselves back is not a good idea for you will only stunt your growth and bring unhappiness upon yourself. The beginning of life is joyful and the ending of life is joyful because there is no true Death. Therefore at every stage of your growth from Baby through to Old age as you see it, rejoice in your being. For you will move forward and be reincarnated and reincarnated. Enjoy this happening. There is an understanding on the Earth Plane that it is a wonderful thing to come off the wheel of life and rebirth. However, once you merge into the oneness there is a longing to go back onto the wheel of life and death for it is a wonderful thing. Therefore understand that it is no better to be complete God, complete Love, complete Joy than to be in an understanding of your own creation as individualised beings. It is all one and you must start to enjoy this. You must start to rejoice within this. Of course there are material circumstances within your Earth Plane that you worry about and you think that you are not doing the right thing by or you move into a place of selfishness and only think about yourself. This is part of the human condition and something that you can overcome. Once you move into the next level of understanding of your consciousness you will Love all at all stages.

This is an important beginning to this book. This is an important understanding that you must comprehend in order to move forward. The majority that are reading this are light workers who wish to further their consciousness, who wish to open up and wish to understand how to open up. Understand that Love is the key to your multi-dimensionality; Love is the key to your moving on as far as your consciousness is concerned. We are here; supporting you, helping you and you will only rise to the higher consciousness of instant manifestation when you move your vessel forward to a point of purity. But the reward for this is bliss, is joy, is happiness, laughter and fun and lightness of being. We welcome you, we love you, this is the beginning, and this is the preparation. To walk forward as Spiritual Warriors, to help the Planet, to help yourselves, to help create everything that you desire, all your abundance, all your joy, all your happiness, all your relationships that will bring you forward through the next fifty years. We are here to support you and we Love you.

This is just the beginning. Rejoice; rejoice in yourselves, we are a higher part of your consciousness. But we are you and we are easily attainable, for that is part of your design, it is in your DNA, it is in your consciousness already. We will open you up; we will give you the tools to open yourselves up. And we will always be here for you. We have unconditional Love for you and the true unconditional Love *is* you. Therefore be brave, be ready to move forward as Warriors of light, of Love.

I am Metatron and I welcome you. I welcome you to your own being. You have come home. You are ready.

I am the Channel that spirit used to bring this information down. It has been my great honour and privilege to be a part of this project. I developed as a medium in a meditation circle years ago. I didn't know about ascension or any of the new age stuff before I developed but I always felt that there was something else in life that I should be doing. Since learning how to channel my life has become much better and I am often astounded by the stuff that comes out. The process is simple, I go into a meditative state and I feel a great loving presence and hear a phrase repeated over and over. As soon as I hear the phrase, I let it repeat a few times so I know it is not just my inner dialogue and then repeat it. After that I just keep on talking and sometimes can still be talking half an hour later. This is all recorded and afterwards I transcribe it. This whole book was written this way and it has been wonderful to feel the bliss that the high vibration brings. I have learned a lot from this whole process and my life is much better for it. I hope that reading this book brings you as much joy and understanding as it has done for me.

Best wishes

Robbie Mackenzie

I am Metatron, I bring you these words with great joy. We are overshadowing this one, and he has done much preparation within his Vessel to get to this point of purity. This is day 20 of his juice fast, he has had no solid food and has been regularly meditating, and praying, purifying and getting rid of negative thoughts. Forgiving himself, the World and everyone that has come into contact with him in order to get to this point of purity. If He did not get to this point of purity, the intense energies that are going to flow through him over the next twenty days would be like putting 10,000 Volts through one of your 60 Watt light bulbs. So understand that if you want to reach to the point of ultimate Manifestation, Power and Channelling. The Highest powers that you can do the most good on this Planet with. You must prepare yourselves; you must clear the negativity from your system. You must forgive and you must walk in unconditional Love. This preparation has not been without it's difficulties and we do not suggest that this process is easy as far as your physical vessel is concerned. But it is simple and with the right action it is easily attainable for you to rise to the heights of ultimate bliss and Love, Peace and Joy. In this state you can channel the heavenly hierarchy.

This one was chosen for his ability to step to the side and purify and accept what is going on within his vessel. But each and every vessel on this Planet, each and every Human Being has the ability to do this, to differing degrees.

As you move forward in your Spiritual development you can be filled with bliss. And as the World Evolves and moves forward and changes, you will become connected more and more with Spirit, with the higher realms.

There is a layer of negativity on the Astral Plane. Which has confusion and whispering of negativity and disruption and confusing Spirits who do not know who they are, for they have not reached for the light. This is where you get an awful lot of your psychic information from in the beginning stages. And there are many who have not purified their vessels that rely on this information and are misled and become tortured Souls because they are not connected into their source. Make no mistake, the Kingdom of God is within you and each and every one of you is able to reach this point of purity.

You are at a point where you are ready, your vessels are ready, and now is the time to walk forward. Now is the time to Ascend, now is the time to expand your consciousness. Now is the time to become the Light-workers that you are designed to become for this transition on the Earth Plane to move forward towards World Peace, World co-operation.

There are many different races on your Planet from different places on your Planet. But you all have the same energy and you will mix together in a melting pot and emerge as true human beings. You are embodiments of Love and you must take off this outer husk of rough armour and move forward with the truth of Spirit. Today is a wonderful day for you to hear these words. For this is you climbing the ladder of perfection, you understanding your own source. Of understanding your own interconnectedness, of understanding who you are and what you are here to accomplish.

There are different levels of consciousness on the planet right now. As you are reading this book, you are ready to make the commitment to join the Army of light that is here to emancipate the planet and to take the steps to clear and purify your vessels. I am your Commander, I command the Armies of light on this Earth plane. I command the many masters that you are walking into becoming. For I am your higher self, so although I command you to move forward, understand that this is your choice to give me the reigns, for I am you. Let go of the control of your lower Chakras. Open up to the balance from your Heart Chakra to the higher Chakras and walk forward as masters of perfection of light, of Love, of truth, of Peace.

This begins your journey.

You must activate your Merkaba's. Your Merkaba is your vessel of light. This is your inter-dimensional vehicle that you must activate so that you may travel and become your 'I am' presence. For when you become your 'I am' presence, you will walk forward as a Master. And then you will be constantly channelling for the connection will be complete and your confidence will increase. This will take effort at first, but you can do this. Have confidence in me if not in your little self to start with for I am here to give you the Power to move forward. I am here to give you the Voltage to expand your vessels. I am here to expand your light. That you may hold more love that you may hold more light. You must service your vehicle every day for this is an experiment in consciousness. And you cannot let your lower self; your vessel and your lower Chakras of your vessel take control. For when you move into your Merkaba and your 'I am' consciousness, your Power among Men, among Mankind will increase. Your Personal Charisma will increase. The weight of your words will increase. Your confidence will increase and your personal power will become immense. This is an important point and you will get to a certain stage – The Ring Pass Not – Where I will decide whether you are ready to ascend to your higher self and completely walk forward as the Master that your husk right now is denying. From that point you will have no inclination to corrupt others in any way. Mentally, Emotionally, Physically, Spiritually, Sexually or in any way dominate in a negative way. But you will have increased Mind Power. You will have connection to all the realms and your D,N,A will be completely activated. You will move forward and you will open up completely and you will feel the effects of this in your vessel, which will be the most amazing thing that you have ever experienced within your lifetime. This will become a regular thing within your vessel when you are ready to walk forward this way and open up to your true potential.

The complete Masters on the Earth plane right now are few. But they will be many. Each Master that walks upon the Earth teeters upon the edge of ascension at all times and can be fed from the pool of God at all times. Your need for sleep will decrease and your need for food will decrease. You must exercise your vessels regularly to keep this vibration high that you may get past the point of the Ring Pass Not. That you will walk forward. This will change you, be ready, and be ready to be re-born into your true selves, open up to that Love, be ready. We will instruct you on how to move forward. Right now your first task is to take away the negativity from your bottom chakras and transcend that energy from your heart and send love to me connecting within to your higher self.

You will all be put on the path and your commanding energy that is Me, that is your 'I am' presence, that is the embodiment of Love will *6/7* become direct and your channelling will become direct from your *6/10* vessels, directly from me. This is a great effort, be brave, be strong and overcome. You are ready; this is your personal Evolution. *2018*

The light has opened up and the forces of darkness on the Earth plane right now are being starved. Are being choked of Oxygen and are dying. The light cannot fail and the Love cannot fail. Your Evolution is moving forward. Nothing can stop this. Understand the Power of your own selves and you can move this forward. If you resist when you know that you are on a Karmic path of service your consciousness will delve into your lower chakras and you will become fearful and worried and in Pain and negativity. This is not something that we want for you. This is not something that we will make happen to you. This is merely part of you looking backwards. This is merely part of you looking towards the past. Towards who you were rather than who you are becoming. To move forward and help the planet and by the Planet we mean Mankind. You must be brave enough to take action every day enough to open up to your own ascension, to your own true path.

Your instruction will be full and comprehensive but we cannot take action for you. You must take action to walk forward into your mastery, to walk forward into your true purpose on this Earth Plane. You are the ones that will make this happen for this is a conscious Evolution. Have confidence.

You will feel the effects on your vessel when you move forward in my direction. This first step to open up your Merkaba is a vital step to understanding your multi-dimensionality. The becoming at one with everything and branching out to what is already there for you. Although we say you are changing you are really becoming more aware of who you are and what you are expanding into. All these branches of your consciousness are already there you are just being made aware of them and in being made aware of them you are walking forward into your power. You must make this a daily practice.

Before you move forward with this you must drink water. Pure, crystal clear water is very important for your vessels for this is part of your design and you are becoming more liquid beings than food beings. A lot of the food on your Earth plane is infused with the essence of the lower Chakras and the Animal vibration. And this has its place. But when you are Ascending, when you are becoming your light body, your 'I am' presence; there is no place for this. And to walk forward fully in your Mastery you must drop this. You must understand the vibration that is going into your body, as well as the vibration of your thoughts and of the higher realms. Every part of your life is relevant and you are moving forward towards impeccability. Therefore you must understand the vibration that goes into slaughtering Animals is not a good one. This is an important point and you will get past a certain point whilst indulging in your carnivorous urges however when you drop this you will Ascend to a much higher place and you will take away the confusion that is brought upon you by the Animal vibration within your body, in your essence.

Purity of thought, word and deed is important for you to move forward. There is no space in the true light-worker for hypocrisy. Therefore understand that everything that you do is reflected back to you and when you come to this point of purity, of excellence, of impeccability, of grace. You will be able to help others ascend and walk into their 'I am' presences. For this is a co-operative, this is a co-operation of Minds, of Souls, of Spirits, of Love, of Truth. You must walk your talk and be brave enough to make the changes within your vessel, in your eating, your meditation, prayer and exercise in your daily efforts to make that difference.

There have been many in the past in your linear time who have taken upon this task by themselves without thousands of other light-workers on the Planet. And they have made great impact as individual Beings. Your Jesus, who embodied the Christ, was an embodiment of perfection and he was worthy. He made himself worthy because of his impeccability to embody the Christ energies and moved the cause forward. Your Guatama Buddha became Buddha through his efforts, through his impeccability and through his understanding of wanting more than merely the material existence. He had everything in the material existence that he could ever want but he knew the truth and the wealth of the Spirit and he sought it. Your Krishna, embodiment of Love, opened up to his understanding of his true nature and moved the cause of spirituality forward. There are examples of light, of manifestation, of ascension and their muse you must take and model your path upon as far as your impeccability is concerned. For this is the level of consciousness that your whole Planet is moving forward towards. They all understood their Merkaba and walked forward with their inner guidance and were emancipated. Truly emancipated and became the Love, the light, the oneness. Became one with the Father, with the Brahman as a Buddha understanding their own essence. And this is the point you are moving forward towards. Do not be deceived that they are higher and you are lesser for there are only different stages of the one and this is an important thing for you to comprehend and assimilate within your consciousness for you to move forward.

The concept of utopia has been discussed and been negated as an impossible dream. However that is part of your design and the understanding of Utopia, of a World at Peace, in co-operation where everybody is considered, everybody is comforted. Is within your reach. But to help move this forward in your linear time and to facilitate a faster change of these energies you must look to yourselves instead of looking to others and become one. Become one with me, become one with your higher selves.

We do not negate your own spiritual tradition no matter which spiritual tradition you come from. Look to the leaders of your spiritual tradition. You do not have to say Metatron for I am them all and they are all me and they understood this therefore do not feel you are being deceived by a different name instead replace Metatron with the name of your chosen deity of your own culture with your own spirituality. This is information to make you a better spiritual Warrior within your own spiritual path. You do not have to break free from the people who you know. You will merely become a better version of that understanding by assimilating the truth of your own being, your own light, your own Love.

Your design is going to push this forward anyway, understand this, the difference in you taking your place and becoming the spiritual Warrior that you are capable of becoming is a matter of time. For the ascension of the Planet is a gradual one, but this is speeded up, by every being that walks into their Mastery. You are being given this opportunity to walk forward on a rollercoaster ride of your own consciousness. This will make life more interesting. Will make your relationships more interesting, more fulfilling. Will make your romantic love affairs much more relevant, much more loving and make your sexual relations much better. Will affect your finances in a positive way when you understand you can manifest all the abundance you need. And will positively affect the economy of the World for all is coming together.

Picture two three sided pyramids, one pointing up and one pointing down, intersecting each other. Picture them spinning in opposite directions. It does not matter which direction they are spinning, only that they are spinning in opposite directions.

Picture this; make it a vivid picture in your mind. Watch it spinning. Now picture yourself in the middle of this double pyramid.

This is your Merkaba. This is the basic shape that taps into the geometry of the universe in order to let you explore the Matrix of creation; In order to let you explore your higher self.

First of all picture this, picture yourself sitting in this double pyramid.

Take a deep breath in, hold, breathe out to the very end of your breath, hold. Only hold for a couple of seconds at first. Then breathe in and breathe out and hold.

Whilst breathing picture your double pyramid spinning around you.

Now put your concentration into the point of your third eye. Bring the picture of your double pyramid with you inside it into the place of your third eye. Now picture a cord going from your third eye to your heart chakra. Picture this as a Golden cord.

All the while breathing in, slowly, holding at the top of your breath. Breathing out, holding at the bottom of your breath: while picturing this.

Hold this vision.

Now expand the love from your heart chakra whilst picturing this in your third eye. Feed this Love and expand this as a bubble of golden Love from your heart chakra. All the Love you have ever felt in your lifetime. For Parents, guardians, siblings, lovers, children, friends, the Planet, conceptions, all the Love.

Expand this from your heart chakra, free this Love, be in this place of expanded Love.

Feel this Love going up the cord to your third eye.

This is the first stage of you opening up your Merkaba. This is a daily routine; you must concentrate on this every day. This is only a beginning. This is you fuelling up your vehicle and getting ready to turn it on. This is you servicing your vehicle and becoming aware that you have a vehicle around you. For you all have this vehicle around you. In the majority it is lying dormant. But we must take this to the next level and spark open your Merkabas. You are at the beginning stage of opening up your Merkabas, opening up your heart charkas, your light, your Love. But this will become easier with the effort that you are going to make. And you will feel the bliss more intensely as you move forward in this understanding.

As you feel the power of your Merkaba igniting you will be moved onto the next stage. Practice this exercise every day. You are going to be given driving lessons to help you not only activate your merkaba, turn on your vehicle, put the ignition on in your vehicle but you are going to learn how to steer it and how to understand where you are going.

Understand, on your Earth Plane, when you go to War you enlist in your armed forces and you are given basic training. You are shown how to operate your weapons and shown tactics and become fit enough to serve and go to war and be worthy soldiers.

This is *your* basic training.

Be brave, for understand that although this Planet will ascend. There is a spiritual war happening on the Earth plane right now. And although the dark forces are merely the grip of the lower chakras amongst humanity, the mental thought forms are clever and it is easy to be misled and deceived. For a lot that is tapping into the Astral plane and the imagination of the lower chakras is very vivid, very real, very warlike and very painful. Mankind is going through the birth pangs of a new understanding, of awakening, of true ascension, which will bring your planet, which will bring mankind into the Utopia that you have been striving for. The difference between this war and your material wars of the lower Chakras on the Earth Plane fought with violence is that you cannot lose. You are already on the winning side, this is your design and although this war is an illusion of the lower Chakras it is a very real experience within humanity. Take it upon yourself to become the master that your design is moving you forward to and you will lead the troops. Your main concern is your own consciousness for when your Merkaba is fully activated your Aura will be all the weapon you need. Keeping your lower chakras from winning the War of consciousness.

In the interim, this is your task, these are your orders, this is your battle plan. Be brave, train, train, train. Practice this meditation and be ready for the next level of your consciousness opening up. We are always with you and we Love you.

This fusion of Power from your consciousness to my consciousness - which is really your higher consciousness, will help you move forward to the higher realms. Understand who you are, your essence, your one-ness, your power, your glory. When you feel this energy completely, when you feel the divine fire and you explode in Love you will understand what is meant by one-ness. We do not mean a sense of well being where you have an inkling that you are part of a greater self. Although this is the beginnings of Samadhi, the beginnings of understanding, the beginnings of awakening and this must be honoured. But to strive for a full disclosure of who you really are, and you are really Me and I am really You but you are of a lesser consciousness and by lesser we mean of a lower vibration.

19

This wonderful melting pot of consciousness on the Earth plane is here to be enjoyed and here for you to be inspired and for you to create the lives that you want to have - for you may have true abundance in this lifetime if you so desire and you put your consciousness towards your Wealth. The true wealth comes from the spirit but from this place of creation you can create Worlds, you can create Universes. You have done already; you are going in and out from a lower vibration to a higher vibration all the time. This is a continuum and this has always been here. Understand the concepts of Love and you will understand all. We are giving you the keys, not only to understand your own consciousness but also to understand the consciousness of the Universe. That Love is your true self and Love is creation.

From your experiences on the Earth Plane where you seeded your consciousness within this experiment of Evolution on the leading, cutting edge environment of creation that the Earth Plane is. You put together the design and we made this Matrix together. I am merely reminding you of the original blueprints that we drew up together. Walk into the confidence, trust yourself, know yourself for to know yourself and to trust yourself is to walk into your Mastery and become who you truly are.

We designed this War of consciousness and let it go so that you may create the experiences that you want to have. Every experience that you see as negative can be overcome. This whole world is transforming but the state that it is in right now is a valid state and must be cherished for its diversity. As you are moving yourselves forward to the point of unlocking your oneness, your truth, you are coming into the point of Revelation, you are being unlocked. We are approaching from the sky that you may ascend. The seals are being unlocked and these seals are your consciousness - the seven seals of your chakras being truly opened up. And the Babylon of your lower chakras of the experience of hate, pain, violence, and negativity will be transcended as you ascend.

Do not judge yourself and do not judge others at all. Do not be at a point of judgement, merely be in your discernment that your consciousness may transform and you will walk into your full power. From this place you may create anything.

There will be a sharing of your wealth for you will see the wealth as belonging to others as well as yourself and we do mean material wealth on this point. Monetary wealth is abundance as well as all the blissful abundance from the spirit. But, the source of your monetary abundance must be from spirit so that you are not led to view the abundance as having power in and of itself, which will lead to greed and negative power. There is a saying that power corrupts and absolute power corrupts absolutely and this is only a truth from the point of the lower chakras. For when you are caught up in your ego's, in your lower chakras, yes, absolute power would corrupt you absolutely. This is why the point of the ring pass not is put in place. That you may ascend past this point because you would destroy yourselves through what is commonly known as the seven deadly sins. They would be your pitfalls and you would fall foul of them. This is not just talking about the power of money. This is about the power of attraction. But when you get to the point of the ring pass not and when you ascend past this point your vessel will be at a point of purity that you may attain absolute power. You may attain absolute manifesting power, absolute healing power. You will be able to bi-locate, you will be able to transcend time and space. You will come to the core of the Universe and you will realize that it is inside you and you will open up to this power. We do not really give you this power. This power is inside you already; you just don't understand how you can access this power while you are in the grip of the lower chakras. But you will transcend and you will ascend and move forward towards your Master being, towards your Avataric self, towards your I am presence, which will afford you the freedom to do what you want to do when you want to do it. This is true abundance and you are moving forward towards this state. The more you purify, the more you forgive and the more you walk forward in unconditional Love the closer you get to the goal.

Your higher self will test you and will put temptation in your way and you will know when it is not a temptation any more. When you can take it or leave it and when you can drop it when you want to. Whichever temptation is in your way that you are getting to the point where although you can have that which is tempting you you will not be a slave to it. This is the ultimate freeing information. Free yourselves, be brave, purify, put on the white cloaks of purity that your book of revelation gives you the understanding of. It mentions the 144,000. This is in reference to your D,N,A. This is in reference to becoming a fully activated human being, all the strands of your D,N,A opening up. Every point of your brain opening up, fully firing, opening up to the consciousness of your human genius. You hold in awe the man Leonardo from Vinci. He was a fully open Human being who came to the understanding of his merkaba early on. Each of you has within you the power to open up to that Universal genius. To the ability to be a Polymath and open up and store and understand and have the wisdom to use that fully open genius and open your D,N,A that you may be a fully useful member of the human race. That you will not hold yourselves back in fear and close down to your small selves controlled by your lower chakras. It will activate both sides of your brain and you will feel the energy pouring into you. You will not be allowed to move past the stage of the ring pass not until you have properly done your basic training. Do not be fooled into thinking that you can take shortcuts within your consciousness. For you made this design, you made this blueprint. And you can only walk into the lift to take you to the next level in your building of consciousness when you have acquired the key to open this door. We are giving you the keys. We are giving you what you need, but you must take action. If you always do what you have always done you will always get what you have always gotten and you will not ascend. And it will cause you pain. For this experiment of consciousness is moving forward. The Angels are helping each and every one of you on the Planet move forward. Do not be fooled that because you are on a spiritual path that you are the only ones that are being helped. All are being helped even the ones stuck in their Violence, even the ones stuck in their Racism, Sexism, ageism and all negativisms that plague your Planet with their greed and corruption. They are operating from their Ego's, from their lower selves and they are in the grip of that point of their consciousness. They need Love, they need the ones who are ready to open up their consciousness, to open up their Merkabas, to open up their Love and expand their Auras. That it will be easier to open their Chakras. For each Master that walks fully into his open enlightened consciousness and taps into the network of Enlightened beings and Avatar on the Planet right now helps those stuck in the illusion of separation. Join in the Joy, join in the party of peace and Love, tranquillity and understanding and come to the peace that passes understanding.

This will be done with effort, so make the effort. This will be done with Love, so Love. Send out your Rockets of Love to all, especially the ones who have wronged you. Love your enemies, for your enemies are a reflection of you that has not moved forward onto the spiritual path yet. Love your enemies, love them as yourself, but be in discernment, you do not have to set up camp and set up home with them (Laughs) this love you send can be from afar. For the company you keep will change and will transform. We do not say this because we are suggesting that you change all your friends but as your vibration raises you will be attracted to ones who are of a higher vibration. For you will feel their bliss and they will feel your bliss and your bliss together will help transcend those that come near. And help your vibration raise that you may get to the point of the ring pass not and transcend it.

The next stage of your Merkaba training –

Do the meditation as you did before. Concentrating on the Golden cord between your heart chakra and your third eye. Do the breathing exercises and continue this for a few minutes.

Take your hands and put your middle finger with your thumb. Hold this up by your side. Transfer your thumb to your index finger. Then back to your middle finger, then your next finger, then your pinky. Then your next finger and your middle finger again.

As you breath in transfer your finger the way we have just shown you. Throughout this whole meditation, change every time you breathe in.

Hold at the top of your breath, breathe out, hold at the bottom of your breath and then change as you breathe in.

Continue this whilst picturing the cord going from your heart chakra to your third eye.

Feel the Love, expand this Love and allow the bliss to flow through you.

Practice this every day.

There are different levels of Mastery that you will achieve. And the more you move forward in your levels of Mastery the easier it will become to see where you have come from and to see where you are going. And what bliss you can assimilate within your being and what effect you have on other people.

There is an understanding on your Earth plane about the hundredth monkey syndrome. Which is an understanding of a mass of people becoming aware of something and it becoming accepted and utilized.

All great truths go through three stages - First they are ridiculed, then they are violently opposed and finally they are accepted as self-evident. Spirituality and the understanding of your mastery is going through the three stages right now. But in order for it to be accepted as self-evident enough people have to assimilate the truth within their being and experience the enlightenment. Experience the raise in vibration; experience becoming Masters and knowing what it is to walk into truth and become one with the all that is. With the Father God, the Tao, Ki, chi, whichever different understanding you need to come to terms with what we are describing.

Many are expecting the critical mass of people to turn the tide on the 21st of December 2012. And this is a wonderful point of spiritual alignment within the Universe and it will be a wonderful thing especially to the light workers who have purified their beings and are ready to assimilate the ultimate bliss and manifesting power of Love. This will be a joyful and happy time. But there are other stages of spiritual evolution on your Earth plane that will experience this time as a point of fear and panic and negativity and will not know what to do or how to move forward and will be stuck in their lower chakras with pain and suffering. Therefore before this date and after that date you must concentrate on your own Mastery that you may alleviate the suffering of the people who are panicking, of the People who are experiencing the negativity. For you, as Masters can alleviate a lot of pain, a lot of suffering. You can affect a lot of healing and you can make a big difference, a big impact. The true light-workers that we have mentioned - Jesus, Buddha and Krishna have affected Billions. That was only three people, you are many and the critical mass of light-workers that are opening up have the ability to take everybody to the next level.

So when things happen that make you seem as if you are being ridiculed or laughed at. Or when things are being violently opposed. Feel the truth within yourself and know that once the point of the critical mass is properly reached Humanity will accept this truth as self-evident.

Do not look to the past, look to the future, look to your potential. Open up your Merkabas, purify. For you will affect this change for everyone. And the joyful thing about your mission is that your mission is to have fun, is to be in laughter, is to not worry, to trust spirit and trust the Angels, to trust your higher self and be joyful in what you want to move forward towards.

Your Profession is very important for we do not suggest that because you are a light-worker that you all have to be mediums in the traditional sense of the word. To be a light-worker is to be at one with your own spirit and to open up your own joy so that you can laugh and you can Love more fully so that whichever Profession you feel your bliss pulling you towards you can do and you can excel at and you can experience it with the utmost grace and power and transformative momentum that an open Merkaba gives you. In all spheres of life, working for the Government, working in Retail sales, in Catering, in Electronics, in Architecture, Alternative therapies, in the Army and you can be a light-worker in the Army. This may seem like a contradiction when your orders are to be at War and to be on the front line. But to help affect a change you must excel at whatever you do right now. And open to the change for you will morph and you have the ability to be in many different professions. Whichever Profession pulls you in the direction you feel you would be most happy, most blissful – this is Spirit laying out your path before you. But it must be a genuine want. Not a want because someone else has steered you in that direction or said you 'Ought to'. It must be from your own self, from your own joy.

The important thing is how you deal with your own self for as you treat yourself better, as you Love yourself, as you respect yourself and as you open up to the divine Love of the Universe that is your true core. You will find yourself treating others with more respect, more reverence, more Love. And the effects of the Lower Chakras, the seven deadly sins will drop off and you will be much happier within your being. And the outside will become a reflection of the inside and you will enlighten many people just by being there, just by being around them. And in them being in your aura you help to unlock them and they in turn will help to unlock others until you have a fully enlightened society that is completely working together. There will be no trace of War. Conflict will cease to exist for you will see each other in your true light. When you have the immaculate conception of each other you will respect and Love and help them move forward.

This will create more diversity on your planet for when your genius is opened you will amaze yourself as to the wonderful designs that you put on life and how you will beautify your Planet and yourselves. And this harmony will open you up to the Universe and you will be accepted as a Planet ready to join the Galactic Council Fully and you will travel the Universe. But not in your primitive vehicles burning fossil fuel - you will come to a better understanding of Engineering design and your space vehicles will become much more effective and you will truly understand.

Exercise is the next point for it must be in tandem with your meditation of the Merkaba for your vessel is very important and it is important that you exercise it. It is designed for Exercise. This is another thing that should be done every day. Preferably before you meditate and pray, to spark up your Merkabas. For in fine-tuning your vessel it will be fit and ready for you to travel the Universe. It will help for in having a good level of fitness within your physical vessel, chemicals in your body enhance your bliss and make you feel good. You can do this even without meditation, even without sparking up your Merkaba to put you on the path first of all so that you are ready to walk into the bliss more fully and so that you respect yourself, so that you help yourself, so that you emancipate yourself and take yourself to the next level. The true light-worker respects the vessel that they have chosen to incarnate into therefore respect your vessel. Exercise it, make this every day and drink water when you exercise. Push your self; push yourself to the limits of your capability. Whichever vessel you inhabit right now you have no excuse but to exercise it. Your Missions are great and there is no place for laziness. There is no place for over indulging in Sloth. For you to be fully emancipated – Exercise, exercise, exercise, respect yourselves. Do not let the lower Chakras of the world win your battle. For each and every different light-worker has a battle with themselves and all the other lower Chakras that are dominating Humanity on the Earth plane right now will contribute to your obstacles. Treat them not as obstacles rather as stepping-stones for you to conquer and for you to move to the next level. Take Sloth out of the equation and exercise. Push yourself to the limits. There must be periods of rest, we understand this but keep the momentum going. This is an important point for to be in a fully functioning Merkaba all areas need to be considered. Ride the waves of consciousness and accept that although your physical vessel, your body is in a denser vibration than your higher consciousness. It is still relevant and your body is part of consciousness and you can affect a full and complete healing upon your vessel no matter what ailment comes to you. With a proper understanding of your consciousness and how you are creating this reality as you are moving forward. All illnesses from the most chronic to the head cold can be overcome with your consciousness, with your healing. But you must be using your vessel properly.

Using it to its optimum function and potential. Consider this – take Sloth out of the equation.

Your next Merkaba lesson –

Be aware of your Merkaba around you. You do not have to picture this right now. Merely be aware of it from the feeling you have had whilst visualising it around you. Feel the connection from your heart chakra to your third eye.

Expand the love from your Heart to your third eye. Feel this as a golden bubble expanding from your heart chakra.

Free the Love, feel the love and excitement of attraction, the Love and excitement of first love. Feel your heart pounding for your divine counterpart in that moment that makes your heart race and makes you feel giddy. Feel this from your heart chakra, feel this energy, expand this energy from your heart chakra.

Feel this love going from your heart chakra through the golden cord to your third eye.

Breathe deeply but do not stop at the top and the bottom. Just make it a continuous breath in and out.

Feel your heart getting faster, pounding, feel the excitement, feel the butterflies in your stomach, from your solar plexus. Move these butterflies from your solar plexus to your heart chakra.

Expand this love, feel this love getting greater and greater as your love reciprocates your feelings. They love you, you love them - feel the excitement of this.

Feel the longing that you have had in many lifetimes being fulfilled as your divine counterpart comes into your life and fulfils all the romantic imaginings you have had of being the one, feel this.

Open this love, feel this going from your heart to your third eye.

Feel your Merkaba enclosing the two of you as you feel that first flush, first kiss, that first hug, that electric experience.

Feel this love - expand this love.

Now take a deep breath, breath out fully. Do not hold at the bottom of your breath, breath in immediately. Deep and long, feel this bliss - bathe in this bliss.

Breath in, breath out, breath in, breath out - deep long breaths. Feeling the bliss, feeling the joy, feeling the excitement.

Now at the top of your breath make a hole in your lips as if you are going to whistle but do not whistle. Just breathe out through this small hole – the whole breath.

While you are breathing out think the words 'Equal speed'

Full and deep.

At the end of your breath breathe in deeply, feeling the love, feeling the joy, feeling the excitement.

Get to the top of your breath – breathe out again in the same manner all the time thinking 'Equal speed'.

Practice this.

You must be visionary in your approach to life for you are at the cutting edge of consciousness on the Earth plane. As Humanity Evolves it will go to higher and higher levels of consciousness. But this point is simple, this point is easy and well within the reach of each and every one of you on the planet right now. This is not a difficult thing though it takes a concerted effort and an understanding of who you are and how your vessel works, how your consciousness works in tandem with your vessel.

You have the equivalent of a formula one racing car at your disposal but you are pushing it around the track instead of starting the ignition and pushing the accelerator.

Understand the mightiness of your being, for you are mighty beings and you have not even scratched the surface of your potential that will bring you forward and open up everything in this physical life.

Are you not tired of war, are you not tired of suffering, are you not tired of pain, are you not tired of negativity and not getting what you desire and being in argument and frustration?

So do something about it, open up your Merkaba – be motivated. Be in your joy, you do not have to preach to others. You do not have to be in the old paradigm of spirituality on the Earth plane. For that was one of a lot of courage and a lot of sincerity but also a lot of control and a lot of negative dogma that entrapped you and enslaved you. And your idea of faith is not fully understood but the basis of everything that we are saying is within your holy books. It is merely the interpretation of that truth which has been used against you, to control you.

There is a heavenly hierarchy and there is a hierarchy on the Earth plane. However understand that you are just as worthy as the highest vibration and the lowest vibration. Or the highest position of power on the Earth plane or the lowest position of power on the Earth plane and you can rise to the heights of both these understandings through your consciousness. Through you using your mental body the right way. Through you turning on your racing Cars and starting to go at the speed you are designed to go at.

This is an exciting thing for your planet; you must see it as an exciting thing.

When you have opposition from people stuck in their lower chakras in any which way. Stand back; do not be in judgement of them. Do not allow them to affect your consciousness. Act; do not react for the illusion is strong.

Free yourself and do what you want to do. For you can all be in this wonderful change. You can all be in this understanding. Do not hold yourself back because of negative convention. Free yourself mentally, emotionally, physically and spiritually. Move yourself to a higher level. Plug into the matrix.

As you raise your vibration your romantic life will change, if you are already with the partner that you are meant to be with your relationship will get better, stronger. You will become wiser within your relationship. And if you are still looking for that partner when you plug yourself into the matrix. If you properly open up your merkaba you will be introduced to your twin flame energy if they are on the Earth plane at the moment. If they are in spirit you will be introduced to them in a different way and they will serve in a different purpose as to help you move forward in your spirituality. Instead you will be united with a higher soul mate and your relationship will be one of joy, of fun, of passion, of great sexual connection, of great romance and of great intensity and you will make a pair bonding that will last for the rest of your lives. Initially this can be challenging and it is one of the most important things on your spiritual path and must be honoured and in honouring yourself you will be honouring them. Give yourself and them the space and time to assimilate the intensity of this relationship that is coming into your being. And as your vibration raises and intensifies so will theirs and your potential will be multiplied. For a light-worker is mighty and powerful. But a light-worker connected to a higher soul mate or twin flame energy can be ten times more powerful when you are operating from your higher chakras and allowing spirit to flow through you. Allowing my voltage to flow through you and purify yourselves you can reach a higher point of potential - through sacred sex, through sacred communion, through sacred eating, through sacred joining your consciousness and ascending together and spreading this love throughout humanity. You will enjoy yourself much better when you understand this and when you give yourself over to your higher self and emancipate yourself from your vessel. Be brave enough to push your light forward.

Freedom is yours when you put yourself upon this path and put yourselves into the hands of spirit, of your higher self, your higher guidance, and your divine light. Your potential opens up and the light comes in and you live a blessed life in grace, your mission is one of fun and laughter. This is no place for dry dogma or misunderstandings of the spirit. This has to be experiential within your own being. Going through your chosen deity to make sure you are not being deceived and trusting in their power to push you forward to this place of laughter and light and righteousness, for righteousness is doing the right thing by god, by the power that is omnipresent within the universe. - Take your understanding of this and your naming of this and expand that understanding and walk into your power.

Now is the hour, now is the time, this is the clarion call. You are being called, you are being pushed forward, and you are being opened up to the light. You must take the next step and now is the hour. It is an important time in the consciousness of mankind and you have a pivotal role, you are a key player; do not underestimate your importance. And as you move along the path, as you ascend Jacobs ladder you will help others come up the ladder. This is a fun thing, it is explained as a ladder but really it is a fun slide for once you take the courage and emancipate yourself it is a fun slide of your consciousness and you improving your vessel, you improving your mental body, emotional body and your spiritual body and expanding into the light that is you. And this is laughter, this is light, this is triumph. You, when you emancipate yourself are the four horsemen of the apocalypse. There, not to destroy villages, not to cause pain and become the dementors of mankind but to free them and to move them forward. For when people see purity, true purity they have a reflection of their own lower self and initially they cannot handle this and they have to go through a period of unrest and negativity. For this mirror that you show them is the representation of the four horsemen of the apocalypse. It is not a physical apocalypse insofar as a third world war or a nuclear desolation. For the world has been on the brink of this truth many times within the last thirty years in your linear time but it has always been stopped by spirit for this is not part of your plan therefore relax, the world will not be decimated in the physical. For mankind is reaching to a higher intelligence and the option to destroy your selves or emancipate yourselves is here but the destroying of yourselves will be individual it will not be collective. For the many on the Earth plane that are here to emancipate mankind, to save mankind have more power than your nuclear weapons could ever have. Stronger than the greatest power of weapons that mankind could ever conceive of is your consciousness therefore walk into your power, your mighty power and become one with the armies of light that are here to emancipate you. This is a wonderful choice, you will run a gauntlet of your consciousness and you will be tested and you will have a choice to fear or to love. For fear is only love mucked up.

The next lesson in your merkaba –

Breathe as you have been breathing before.

Feel the merkaba around you.

Picture in your mind white light and the love expanding from your heart chakra through the golden chord to your third eye.

Expand this, expand this now more, more than your romantic love to encompass the earth, to encompass mankind, to encompass all the nearly seven billion on the planet.

Connect with their heart chakras.

For there are ones that are emancipated and ones that are not emancipated but connect with them all for all have the capacity for unconditional love.

Connect with them all, feel love for each and every one of them, this has to be unconditional - feel this expanding from the earth out to the universe, to all universes, to all consciousness.

Feel your vessel starting to power up.

Now, think in your mind 'equal speed' repeat it 'equal speed'.

Feel the energy getting faster and faster as you connect into the consciousness of the universe and all the universes.

Now repeat in your mind 'Nine tenths the speed of light' – 'Nine tenths the speed of light'

Feel your vibration raising – Feel Love, Expand the Love.

Now breath in a deep breath.

At the top of your breath purse your lips as if you are going to whistle and blow out quickly without whistling.

Make the hole small so that the air comes out of your mouth slowly but with power down through your whole breath.

As you do this picture immense white light and Golden love coming from your heart chakra.

Expand this – Blow all the way out with this breath.

Feel the Love and expand the Love.

Feel the light, bathe yourself in this light as you make this happen.

Be ready, be ready to overcome fear with love. At the point of emancipation you will have to choose between fear and love. This is the testing point – the take off point of your Merkaba.

Be ready, practice this every day.

We Love you and are with you through this whole emancipation process.

No fear, only Love – Expand it.

Be ready.

This is the moment of tribulation where you must let go of all past vows from all past lives to bring you forward into the present, into the moment so that you can live in the now and you can emancipate your vessel, your psyche and your consciousness.

You have been here many times before on this Planet but you have also travelled. You do not understand the depths of your soul and your past lives. These will be opened up to give you a better understanding of who you are. And when you come to the concept of a higher timeline, a higher concept of time. A higher concept of how you have actually created everything around you, you will be emancipated. This is the point of tribulation, this is the point of freedom and this is the point where you walk fully into your mission.

Take upon this vow and replace the beginning with your chosen Deities names.

'Metatron I ask of you to clear all my past lives vows and negative Karma. You are working with the Lords of Karma who will balance my Karma and allow me to walk fully into my Merkaba and be freed and take me in this incarnation to the next step to help Mankind Ascend, to help Mankind change their consciousness to a higher level of understanding that the Planet may work together.

This is my wish, this is my vow and this is my command to the Universe.

I walk into my mastery now and I seek only love and light and truth and seek to fully activate all the strands of my D,N,A. All my Chakras and my higher chakras, the left and the right side of my brain, the ida and the pingala and root myself within this Planet that I may help Ascension and be a lighthouse to others and beam my light.

I ask this in Metatrons name Amen'.

Replace my name with your chosen Deity so that you feel comfortable within this Vow but this is important that you clear the past in order to clear the future. In order to walk forward and be all that you can be and emancipate yourself and be strong and powerful and in your mastery and at that point you will move past the ring pass not. This must be in sincerity for if there are any lower chakra issues that are getting in the way of this you will not pass the ring pass not – you will not be able to.

Put yourself on the path, emancipate yourself, this is the time and this is the place. Now is the hour – **this is the Clarion call.**

You have chosen this mission; if you did not choose this mission you would not be reading this.

Synchronicities will flood your existence as you begin to trust the Universe.

2012

We have worked with one who has channelled screenplays for you and brought you an understanding of religion and spirit and love and truth and the Angels through Films and the Power of the Jedi, which was channelled. The understanding of being a Jedi is the understanding of being a light-worker however the lightsaber and the violence are merely the spiritual warfare within your psyche, within your consciousness. Not the physical violence within the films although we understand this is exciting for you but this is here for a reason, be that Jedi, be that Warrior and understand yourself and trust the force. For the force is within you and illuminating everything within the Universe, within the consciousness and within all the dimensions, the higher dimensions and as you raise your vibration you will be able to taste of these higher dimensions and these higher dimensions are wonderful. Within your lower chakras you depend upon artificial stimulants through drink and drugs and food and additives and this has its place as far as your exploration of the material world is concerned however when you raise yourself to a higher vibration and you taste of the essence of the higher dimensions it puts all different highs of your material world to shame. For there is nothing better than the divine nectar of the higher dimensions as experienced through a lower vibrational creature reaching to a higher vibration. This ecstasy, this Joy, this Amrita, this taste of pure bliss, of pure pleasure, pure unadulterated joy can only be experienced through raising your consciousness to the higher levels. And when you have a taste of this you will not be attracted to any of your lower forms of stimulant. For you will understand that this higher vibration and higher dimensional energies and nectar can give you everything and more and is side effect free apart from the fact that you will become more healthy in mind, body and spirit and you will be able to move forward with the ambitions of your passion which will emancipate your abundance and will bring in your joy and free you. This is the reward for the light-worker, this is the reward for your discipline, for your compassion – pure love, as you have never experienced it before for it is deeper and wider and stronger and higher than you can even comprehend right now. And this is the moment that you can reach for that light, reach for that truth, reach for that Love. Your Merkaba will take you and emancipate you once you have passed the ring pass not all is here for you. The World is here for the taking, all the joy, all the peace, all the love, all the truth that you could have ever imagined and your brain will open up, your consciousness will open up. For make no mistake your consciousness is not your vessel, your vessel is merely a receptacle and a filter for you understanding your creation of yourself within this incarnation and it has its place and it is also divine. But open up your consciousness so that you can walk into the adventure that *is* your consciousness.

We rejoice in your emancipation, we love you and look forward to you joining the higher orders. The Ruby Order and the Saphire order are open ready and waiting for your initiation. Walk forward as a Master, join in, have a say in where this Planet is going. For make no mistake, your Governments and your Political Hierarchies and your financial structures and your Illuminati (Laughs) think that they are controlling the destiny of the Planet. Do you not understand that their higher selves are controlling them - in subtle ways. You are not moving forward towards Slavery, you are moving forward towards emancipation. Trust this; do not judge anyone on the Earth Plane – not one. For in judging you will be judged through the law of cause and effect and you will bring instant Karma upon yourself. Be pure in your thought; be led by your spirit. Open up to the Force, open up to the Light, Become this Warrior. Your gifts will open up and your personal power will be immense. But the key to this is Joy; the key to this is Love. Trust yourself, and I AM YOU, therefore trust me.

It is time for you to be taken to the next level of your consciousness. You are being opened up subtly and the words we have spoken so far have subtly affected your subtle bodies and are gently opening you up to the truth of who you are. When you feel this deeper within your being you will know the time has come to move to the next level. We speak of food, we speak of exercise, we speak of meditation, we speak of purity and all these things are important but a willingness to open up your consciousness is even more important and to not fear. This is why we say to replace your traditional Deity for the name Metatron for the name does not matter but the Power matters for we are all one – understand this. I am one with you the same as all the other Deities are one with you no matter which one you have traditionally been brought up with it is important that you open up your consciousness through the truth of who you are. This is important, an important point for you can do all the exercise, all the meditation and eat the right things but if you do not willingly accept the truth of who you are you will not move forward you will simply be in fear and fear is a big block towards your emancipation. Drop fear, fear is of the lower chakras, fear is negative. Healthy discernment is where true spirituality lies. Discernment is different from fear yet brings in judgment without bias. This is you walking into your mastery and is a very important point to make for you are emancipating yourself so you can see things from the Eagles view. And when you see things from the Eagles view you can see the whole landscape. This is important for to see where you are going you must know where you have come from but not look backwards. Only look forwards, the Eagle does not look backwards when he is flying he only looks forward and he flies to great heights. Be as the Eagle, soar above earthly concerns. This is an important point.

true Christ Spirit. This is what was meant and this is what must be assimilated. If in that particular religion you consider yourself born again ponder these words. If you are of a different tradition these words still hold firm for the truth of the light is inherent in all religion. But it has been masked and it has been overshadowed by Mans greed and quest for domination and dominion over others.

You must get and forget, you must give and forgive. Your joy will be true creation and you will be able to manifest everything and anything. Get to that point of true spirituality and no matter which religion the ones who are in charge of the religion if they are walking the talk of their own spirituality will look up to you and will join forces with you and we will emancipate the World in a Spiritual way no matter the tradition all over the Globe in all traditions.

I am here to Command the forces of light, which go under all names that understand the truth of the one. All true religions that understand the truth of the one. All true powers of the higher spirit that understand the truth of the one. Therefore be strong, be bold. Do not try to change anyone merely change yourself and your power will be evident. Your power will emancipate many and the more you emancipate the more will be emancipated that will be able to emancipate others and we will reach the point that we are meant to reach, the point that all the seers have seen which is true about the end of the World for the end of the World is coming. The end of the World is nigh. But this is the end of the World, as you know it with negativity and corruption and untruth. This is the point we walk forward into a new World, into a new light, into a new age. And the Devil is not only locked up for a thousand years as was prophesised but is completely destroyed within your psyche, within your consciousness and is freed and you are freed from the grip of fear. Therefore be strong and accept your mission and this is to work on yourself and NO ONE ELSE. For once you work upon yourself you will be led to where you need to go to fulfil your mission to help others. But this will not be to preach; this will be to show the way. Once you have passed the ring pass not you will walk into your power and you will be truly unstoppable for nothing can stop this. Nothing can stop the force of God, nothing can change the will of God and this is something that is fixed within Humanity. This is something that is fixed that cannot be denied. This is something that is fixed that will not be denied. And it is unstoppable, this is a freight train of power moving forward and the resistance of mankind is a mere dried twig on the track. Understand this Power, join forces, and work on yourselves. Meditate, pray, purify, walk into your joy. Understand the joy that you can have as a fully emancipated Human being. You will be able to learn different languages. You will be able to assimilate, take in much more information and be able to use that information. Your powers of communication will expand and extend and you will walk forward without fear of anyone on the Earth Plane for you will be blessed and protected. For the truth of it being said that the Lord protects his own. You are all his own but when you understand that when you walk forward in your higher Chakras you walk into that Power and that is what was meant by this. The Lord protecting his own is

—

46

understanding that when you walk into your own spiritual armoury, when you walk into the shields that are around you and that you can put on that are as light as a feather and accept the wings that take you to a higher point of consciousness within your Merkaba you are fully protected. This has to be without violence, without bias, without hatred, without fear, without any negativity. And this is not an unreachable point, this is a point of inevitability, this is the inevitability that you will move forward with. Take up your mantle of truth, be as gentle as a Lamb for your truth and your love and your power will calm the savage beast and the savage beast of the lower chakras of all mankind will be calmed in your presence. Be true to yourself and your light. For this is your mission, this is the moment you take up the mantle. This is my Clarion call to all Light-workers, this is my Commandment. This is you becoming one in gentleness, in mighty Power, in meekness and you shall inherit the Earth and the old ways of violence, of twisted negativity and manipulation will be dropped as an outer husk and you shall conquer all and it will be worth it so you must make the effort to open up your consciousness and become one with me. Join the Forces of light, be motivated and walk forward in your truth and your Power. This is the moment, this is the Clarion call, and this is the twinkling of the eye. Free your self, practice every day. See the effect of the lower chakras from others as just what they are and be joyful and compassionate and loving to them. Do not argue with them, bring back your light for you will be led to mix with people of the light, of the emancipation and you will be helped and encouraged and you will feel free and you will be able to fly high as the Eagle in your consciousness and soar above all the negativity. This is your mission, this is your point of emancipation and we are Joyful that you are reading this.

Take up arms, your responsibility is to yourself for in clearing the negativity within you and coming to that point of purity everything will change in your outer World. And you will have more opportunities; more doors will be open to you and the excitement of what you are doing, what your joy is, what your passion is will become motivated towards great success. And you will understand and recognize those that are here to help you. And understand and recognize those who are here to try to put obstacles in your way. But they are merely here as stepping-stones for you to emancipate yourself from. And in emancipating yourself from them and not judging them, not including your-self in their Karma. You will help them emancipate themselves. This is the truth of your being, allow yourself to be excited about this moment and open up and accept the consciousness of the Hierarchy of light.

This is the sword that was brought to divide - that was brought by the Christ light. It is here to divide, not to cause negativity or consternation or argument. But to cause a divide in your understanding of what is for you and what is here to hold you back. And you may walk forward with this sword of emancipation, with this Jedi Saber - Saber of light that is here to help you, this is to free you from the Jihad of War. For that war is within you, free yourself from this. Use the Sword, divide the negativity, do not be a Hypocrite for in your Hypocrisy you will only chain yourself.

We Love you and are with you every second, every moment, we are part of your very consciousness and Our Power is readily accessible when you accept who you are and walk forward in your Power.

The next step in bringing yourself into your Mastery is to forgive. To come to the place of unconditional Love and truth within yourself and concentrate upon your heart chakra as you have known it in a romantic sense as well as the love for your family and friends etc. Now we must expand this and walk into unconditional Love and understanding that everyone that you have negativity for or you sit in judgement of are only at a certain part of their evolution, their growth. You would not judge or despise a Baby for messing it's nappy (Diaper). You would help the Baby and know that this is part of it's growth. You would not judge the Baby for you understand this is part of growing, part of life. Therefore become the Adult. Although it is not your responsibility to change the nappies of Mankind It is your responsibility to not sit in judgement over them. Or to have any negativity for the negativity will not add to their Karma, it will add to yours and will prevent you from moving forward. This is the place of maturing into the fully emancipated Human being and you must take this for everybody on the Earth plane. You are not here to sit in judgement - this is the point.

So, this next exercise with the Merkaba is of unconditional love, which will open your heart fully when you let yourself go of your judgements and your negativity. For those who Murder, who hate, who spread Fear amongst Mankind and even on your Planet there are still people that eat other human beings. Cannibalism is still a thing on your Earth plane. Do not fear this but do not judge it for this is a certain stage and you must send out love to them for that is the only way that they are going to be more quickly emancipated. This is the way to transformation and this is the next step in your Merkaba - for to launch your Merkaba properly you must be in unconditional Love for all of Mankind. You must practice the exercises we have already given you but this is when you will launch your ship of pure light and travel the Universe of consciousness and be able to go between the dimensions, walk into your full and pure Mastery and take your place in the Galactic Council. For each individual that emancipates themselves will have a say in the change of consciousness and be part of the one that will open up to a greater understanding of who really controls the growth and the well being of the Universe.

You will be introduced into the Galactic Council and it's Members who are part of you and you are part of them. And there will form a higher council on the Earth plane. This already has a basic template in your United Nations but it is not being fully honoured, fully respected, fully appreciated and fully used yet. But it will be and this will be the ruling force that will bring into line all the laws on your Earth plane. And there will be an amalgamation ultimately and a one World Government. But this will not be ruled through Fear, this will be ruled through Love, truth and respect. The World will be truly emancipated.

This time is vital, take your place as a Master to help this move forward for this is important and again we reiterate – the greatest work you have to do on this Earth plane is on yourself and keep your pure light for once you are plugged in, once you are tapped into the Matrix you will be led and your consciousness will expand. - You will be led by the light, but the light *is* you. Therefore do not allow yourself to be trapped in your lower chakras, emancipate yourself.

Now, thinking of your Merkaba, picturing it around you with a golden cord going from your heart to your third eye.

Picture your chakras.

Picture the route going from your Heart chakra down into mother Earth and from your Heart chakra up into the Universe.

Feel the Love for all Mankind – Send the Love to all. Send the Love especially to the ones who have treated you negatively as a whole in Mankind. All the dictators, all the ones who stand and rule by Fear, all the ones who Murder and manipulate. Send them Love, send them compassion, send them light. Look on them from a mature point of view and understand that they are merely messing their nappies, love them for they too are children of the light.

Now take this time line, for your linear time does not count within your Merkaba therefore send love back, send love to those who have committed the greatest atrocities. Bathe in this love of non-judgemental unconditional love. Bathe in this truth, emancipate yourself and emancipate them and you will heal the past and heal the future and the past and the future will become one for as it is above so it is below. Feel this within your Merkaba, feel this spinning. Tree May 29 ✳
Terri Schwartz

Feel Satan at your Doorstep, feel Lucifer ready to cause you harm, ready to cause you fear but do not Fear, Love. Do not Fear, LOVE, DO NOT Fear, only LOVE. Emancipate yourself for you are stronger than Satan, you are stronger than Lucifer. And the Angels, even the Dark Angels can do nothing without the will of God therefore understand that God only wants your Emancipation and the Angels of Dark and the Angels of Light are here to serve you, are here to emancipate you.

Go through this Initiation – DO NOT FEAR. Do not Fear any Bodily harm, Emotional harm, mental harm. Feel that negativity wanting to take over you but do not give into it, LOVE IT. Love all that has happened before in the name of evil with an understanding that you are stronger than this, that you have more Love than this, that you have more power than this, that this can not break you.

Emancipate yourself from the Devil - emancipate yourself from Lucifer.

Love, for all is one, the dark and the light are one – become one with everything.

Love it, love all, free yourself, walk into truth, this is the point of your Merkaba opening up and you being transformed into a being of light. Into the being who you truly are, into the being that will help mankind emancipate themselves and walk into the next point of their evolution.

This is the most important point of teaching in light-workers to understand that you are not being fooled, that you are being freed.

Love, Love, Love.

This energy will come upon you more and more and it will help you break free from the shell of negativity.

This is the Lucifer Initiation. This has been much misunderstood. You are a being of light, you can overcome your lower chakras, you can overcome Lucifer, and this is the point of you breaking free. This is the point of you moving from illusion to illumination. This is you becoming the Illuminati, but not the Illuminati that the lower chakras would have you believe of the conspiracy theorists that are trying to manipulate mankind. This is the true Illumination of mankind, the true Enlightenment, the truth, the power and the glory that will transform you and you will become an illumined one and in walking forward in this understanding your power will be granted to you and all the gifts will open up and you will be freed. Allow your self to bathe in this understanding and free yourself from the heavy husk of illusion that is on the Earth plane. This is your point of light, this is your point of understanding, and this is you freeing yourself from the dark one for you are becoming the yin and the yang. You are assimilating the dark and the light and becoming one with everything. For love has no sides, there is no right side and no wrong side, there is merely the evolution of your soul therefore understand you can not lose and while you are in duality consciousness taking the side of the light and truly walking forward in your emancipation will be you having an understanding of the light and the dark being one. This is the most important thing that you will ever assimilate within your vessel as a Human being and once this is properly, truly and wholeheartedly assimilated and you are emancipated, you will join with the Galactic Council and your consciousness will expand. You will have the peace that passes understanding and the power of the light.

These commands we give are not as a Dictator would give with drastic consequences if not obeyed. You have free will and this is the wonder of creation, of the universe, of the human condition and the ability to rise above your lower self, Evolve and move forward. These Commands I give are from your higher self to yourself urging you to move forward. Therefore do not feel as if you are under pressure that you are being manipulated or dictated to for this is simply not the case. You rising above your lower chakras, rising above the influence of the vessel, which holds you down - Will free you.

These Commands are the true Commandments of your higher self as was the commandments when Moses channelled the messages that came through for the Ten Commandments. These were your higher self reaching out to your lower self and saying of course it is better if you live in a respectful society where you do not Kill, where you do not covet others possessions for that is being in a competitive energy of consciousness. Now the difference between being in a competitive energy of consciousness and being in a creative energy of consciousness is one of tapping into your higher self, For in competition there will always be conflict and will always be feelings of inferiority and superiority which lead to war, to violence, to negativity, to pain and to suffering. Instead, when you tap into your higher self, the matrix of creation and spark up your Merkaba you are no longer in competition with anyone for you understand that you *are* everyone and in understanding that you are everyone you can create and you can share the wealth and there is no need for jealousy, there is no need for envy, there is no need for worry about others having more than you or you having less or being less or being more. So understand your higher self is moving you forward. My Commands are your higher self, which wants the best for you. In moving forward in your creation, in understanding that you are powerful creators and by this we do not just mean abundance coming in and you becoming 'lucky'. This creation is all encompassing. The little selves do not understand the larger selves that are there ready to take on the mantle of power, of strength, of manifesting abilities – But you will.

Therefore accept the commands as a gentle truth and follow the barometer of your bliss that will move you forward to create all that you need to create. Do not be in competition with anyone, the only competition you should ever have is with yourself, against yourself striving for constant and never ending improvement of yourself. For when you strive to improve yourself you tap into your core and your core is perfect dear ones, understand this, you *are* perfect. This is an important point for you to comprehend. Your true essence is perfection, you are moving back to that truth and that experiential understanding. For you are divinity, you are God; you are the essence of the Universe. In your individualised state, in an un-evolved way you find it hard to comprehend this truth but assimilate this and you will move forward and you will be great creators with power and you will lead others forward to their truth. Open yourselves up – this is the point of truth, of manifestation.

As you read this we are overshadowing you, as you read this we are moving you forward, as you read this we are opening you up, opening your D,N,A up. Opening every strand up that you may be as your design intended you to be. Make no mistake, this is true and this is happening. Allow yourself to feel our energies, allow yourself to raise your vibration, allow yourself to move forward and purify. For this is the moment, this is the twinkling of the eye.

We wish to introduce you to the higher Council, the Galactic Council that governs the Universe. It is true that you can visit the Galactic council with your consciousness and you can open up to the truth of the wider Universe not only within your consciousness but on the physical plane also. For it is true you have been visited many times on this Planet by beings that you consider to be extra terrestrial or Aliens as you put it. However you must come to the understanding that there is no such thing as an Alien for you are all points of creation from the same essence, from the same core, from the same Matrix that was created for this Universe. You are not alone in the Universe, the physical Universe, this three dimensional Universe. You are visited regularly. There are many among you that understand this truth and know this truth and yes, your governments have covered this up. But this has been because you were not ready before to understand, comprehend and assimilate this truth. There is a certain point of flowering within your consciousness that you have to realise before you can come to terms with this. There is a general understanding that there is - 'something else that is there and when you consider the vastness of the Universe it would be arrogant to suggest that you are the only beings in the Universe'. This truth will be widely accepted as you move forward to become part of the galactic Council. And your technology will improve as intergalactic relations improve and are spread wider on your planet. The consciousnesses of all the beings that visit your planet are not always past the ring pass not however the majority are. You are moving towards a time of understanding the difference between what is from the essence and what is from the vessels perspectives, even of these visitors to your planet. Your part in this transformation of understanding is to purify your vessel that you may be able to walk forward and transmit the energies of light that need to be transmitted in order to transform this world. This is an important understanding to come to terms with.

There are many different extra terrestrial beings that are very benevolent and wish the best for the Earth and they come in peace and help spread their technology, spread your understanding, evoke and help move forward your spirituality and spiritual gifts and they come in Love and have been coming for thousands of years. In sparking up your Merkabas and widening your consciousness you will be prepared for this wider truth and you will be able to travel, not just in your consciousness but physically across the Galaxy. You must be ready for this; this is part of the change and part of why this book is being channelled right now. To prepare you ready, for the World is coming to an end – as you know it. And the widening of your consciousness is going to transform this. The technological revolution will astound you when you understand the technology that has been all around you for Millennia. But there are still many problems to be solved. You, as the light-workers, as the spiritual warriors, the Jedi of the Universe, are being equipped with the tools that you may Liaise with all the beings in the Universe and you may bring your Planet forward that you can be let in and the wider truth of what your planet has been used for.

We do not wish to see the World descending into negativity and your design is leading you to a positive place. But the Earth needs to be habitable. This is part of the drive that your Eco Warriors and the consciousness that is changing on your Planet as far as your pollution of the Earth's atmosphere is helping. Do not fool yourself into thinking that you are saving the Planet for the Planet will survive in the physical. What is important to understand is the more you pollute your atmosphere, the closer you are to bringing your own physical Armageddon and choking yourselves to death. This is the real meaning that your eco Warriors need to fully comprehend for the Earth will survive. If you destroy yourselves physically the Earth will flourish and other beings will be seeded upon this Earth. This is another point that your Seers have seen and predicted the other level of Armageddon. This is not where your Planet is going, but understand that this is an experiment in consciousness and your free will is an important gift. Without it, it would not be an experiment in consciousness. If you get to the point where you pollute your Earth so much, Humanity will still survive but it will only be the light workers who are taken from the planet before it is re-seeded. Therefore understand in taking up the mantle of the light worker, fulfilling your design and consciously walking forward, opening up your Merkaba, being at one with your truth and tapping into the Matrix you are ensuring your survival. All are loved on the planet but all have free will on the planet also. Help everyone make it through ascension, take on the mantle of the Warrior that you are, take on the perfection of your truth. This may sound dramatic, and in the physical, three dimensional, linear understanding it is dramatic. This is part of your reality just now. But the higher truth of spirit is that nothing really dies, there is only transformation. The old ways, the lower consciousness does not have a place anymore. This is why it is dying out, this is why the light is strangling it, this is why you are here reading this text - You are ready.

We say none of these things to instill fear; we only speak the truth to inspire action. And you will be inspired when you appreciate yourselves for who you are and the joy of this mission is that we wish you to be happy, to be in laughter and fun and passion and to follow your dreams and not allow others to hold you down or be in enslavement to the negative consciousness of energy stealing, the negative consciousness of self-aggrandizement, the negative consciousness of superiority or inferiority. That is the old consciousness; open yourself up to the new consciousness for you are being led and loved. And the ones that choose to destroy themselves will die off physically but their consciousness will change and they will be re-incarnated again therefore do not feel sorry for anyone who chooses that negative path merely open yourself up to the positive path that will help them and help you. Do not even consider it, do not judge them for all that are on an evolutionary path have been on that negative plane, in that negative consciousness and had those experiences many times in many lifetimes. This is a part of the matrix of creation – of experience. And it is worthy for what it is but there is a time and a place for everything in this Universe, in this linear time creation and your Planet is at a point of blooming, flowering, of being ready. You are at the forefront of this understanding of consciousness. Do what your higher self is commanding you to do and not only will you be in joy and enjoying your life but you will be much more powerful and you will be able to enjoy this Planet while it is able to sustain you with Oxygen.

The next step in your awakening is one of action; you must put these things into action. These are not empty words we speak; these are the truth of creation. When you accept yourselves you will be opened up and it will not be the groups of people who are trying to manipulate the Earth for their own ends who will win out in the end. It will be the light workers who wish the best for all that will truly govern the Planet in cooperation with the higher Galactic Council. Understand the importance of your missions, the importance of reading this, the importance of us overshadowing you while you read this that you may take in and assimilate everything that you are being given. For what is being asked of you will create a whole new Paradigm for the Earth.

Prepare, prepare, prepare.

As your consciousness opens up you will become more aware of people's motivations and you will see through them more clearly when they are not being truthful with you or how they will move forward themselves and their manipulations. And your manipulations will drop as you move forward in purity and allow yourself to open up to your light. This is the mark of the true light worker. Seeing the truth and seeing the manipulation and the negativity but not judging it and seeing it for what it is. This will take you to the next level and help you move forward. We are excited at this time in Humanity on the Earth plane for we know there will be a continuation of the Human race and if you have to be removed from the Planet you will come back here again when it is habitable. This is not the direction that we hope for you but you are assured of the continuation of the human race. There are enough people of a higher consciousness to bring forward your species to the next level and with concerted effort and Love you may stay on this Planet and you may all raise your consciousness together as you go through the gateways leading to the emancipation of your kind.

We wish to give you a new Prayer, a new awakening understanding of what it is to tap into your higher self through prayer, meditation and concentrated effort of will which is effective Prayer. You may replace Metatron with your chosen Deity.

"Lord Metatron, I ask to be taken to the next level, I ask for divine protection in all that I do. I ask for my abundance to be brought forward to me. I ask for all my Karma to be cleared and I ask for my Prayers to be answered. I ask for my meditation to be successful. I ask to be led in the right direction, may I have the Synchronicities that I may join with my own soul group and be raised to the higher level. I ask that I be pointed in the right direction to eat the right things, drink the right things, speak the right way and act according to my design that the plans of the Heavenly hierarchy are fulfilled. I ask that my abundance benefits others and my actions speak louder than my words but that my words are pure, sweet and enjoyable. I ask to take my place in the Galactic council and that I am made worthy and the husk of negativity is taken away. I ask that all that I say and do is in alignment with divine will and that I become my divine self so that I may walk forward into my mission and that I have the energy, strength and power to fulfil my mission. I ask that my active and passive side join together in my Merkaba and that I am fully emancipated.

I ask this in your name, Amen"

This is a prayer to use before going into your Merkaba meditation that you may be truly enlightened and that you become the Deity, the embodiment of love, the embodiment of truth and at one with the ocean of divine love. This is your potential. After saying this Prayer go into your Merkaba meditation. Go through the meditation the way we have shown you. While picturing your Merkaba around you ask for the Violet flame to be brought upon your whole being. Your Mental body, your Emotional body, your Spiritual body and your Physical body. This is working in conjunction with Archangel Zadkiel.

While picturing your Merkaba around you from the core of your heart chakra repeat the mantra. –

'I am the Violet Flame, I am the Violet Flame, in action in me now I am the Violet Flame. To light alone I bow I am the Violet Flame. In mighty cosmic power I am the light of God shining every hour. I am the Violet Flame blazing like a Sun. I am Gods Sacred Power freeing everyone.'

Whilst doing this and picturing your Merkaba spinning, the Golden cord going from your Heart chakra to your third eye. Place your consciousness in the position of your third eye. And you feel the Love coming from your heart chakra.

From this place you may visualise yourself moving forward, you will open yourself up and the initial energy when you take off will be of becoming one with the Universe and you will experience the divine light, you will experience the divine love, you will open up to the truth of yourself. From this place within your third eye is your Cockpit, your driving place and where you are to place your consciousness and you will be filled with light and your whole body will move forward in light, love and truth and after you have exploded in love, after your consciousness has moved forward you will be able to use your Merkaba as the vessel which will turn into your spaceship which you will be able to explore the Universe with. The next Merkaba lesson will be how to steer your Merkaba from sitting in the place of your third eye. You must picture these things all at once whilst doing your merkaba meditation.

The Violet Flame will take you to the next point of purity. Will purify the love that you have been exercising, that you have been practising within your merkaba that will fully fuel you. When you understand how to do this and when you feel the truth of this within your vessel you will never run out of this fuel. Your life is going to change dramatically for the better and from this place your manifesting power will become immense and you will be able to link to the Galactic Council. We are waiting for you in the Galactic Council ready to welcome you. Once you pass the ring pass not, once you open up your consciousness, once you move yourself forward. We are awaiting you with open arms and open hearts in love ready for you to take your place to oversee the emancipation of your Planet, the emancipation of the consciousness of your people. You getting to this point excites us, we are excited by you moving yourselves forward with the opening up of your consciousness and we are ready to gift you with the gifts of the spiritual warrior fully. Once you come under control of this you will not look back.

Initially in opening up your Merkaba until you are under control of this energy you may notice your electrical field affecting the electrical appliances that you have in your houses and your places of work or around you you may see the lights dimming and some things may even blow up, light bulbs blowing. This is why it is important that you master the merkaba meditation that you may pull this power forward. This is why it is important that you practice, practice, practice so that you are in control of your energies and you do not negatively affect anything, and do not negatively affect yourself, the power of this is immense and we are leading you forward to embody this power, this light, love and truth.

From this you will be opened up to the Akashic records. You will be opened up to the divine blueprint of the Planet and all that has happened before and all the future possibilities. You will be opened up to the halls of Amenti and in this expansion of consciousness you will be able to lead mankind forward in full integrity and all your endeavours will blossom. Your path will become clear, clean, straight and laser focused and the amount of work that you will accomplish will increase, be ready, and be strong.

Practice, practice, practice.

You are sowing seeds of hope and you will reap a harvest of love, this takes effort but you have everything that you need. Do not be afraid of your mission, walk into your power, and walk into your multi dimensionality. Open up your Merkaba - spread the light. Your creativity will expand and you are ready for this expansion. Trust your inner barometer, trust your own power, the way you gauge yourself and keep pushing the envelope of your own consciousness. This is an important teaching, important for you to take it in and assimilate it and take action upon it. For this is you being ready.

Awaken dear ones to your potential; awaken to all the love that we are bringing with you. I may seem like a hard taskmaster but you will thank me for pushing you forward, for being there coaching you, informing you, loving you. I see the potential of each and every one of you that is reading this and although the one who is channelling this is solitary right now we have the names of each and every one of you that is reading this, Know that you are in the Army of God, the Army of light and you are being armed with everything that you need. For all that you will need is your Merkaba, all that you will need is your expanded aura; all that you will need is your Love. I am speaking to you personally and I love you. But your time, your linear time is moving forward and time is of the essence, when you hear this take control of your lower chakras, open up your merkabas, be ready to move forward, be ready to move into the driving seat of your ship, be ready to transport your consciousness, be ready to help heal the planet, Practise what I have given you, be brave.

You are the warriors that are going to defeat the darkness and in you transcending this duality you have already won this battle, you have already won the war. Be brave enough to open up to your truth, to open up to your light.

This message will reach the far corners of the World and that is part of your mission to help this message reach where it is meant to reach. To discern when you see a light worker that is ready to open up their merkaba to ask for the divine guidance of myself, of the Galactic council, of your chosen deity that you may lead them in the right direction and they may open themselves up, you will inspire many.

Your biggest mission is to be in joy, is to have fun, is to let go of the fear, is to allow yourself to be at one with your spirit and feel the excitement of all your chakras opening up. For everyone who moves forward wholeheartedly without denial of their true self I will implant a diamond light in your heart so that you will have the motivation to fulfill your mission. You may ask this from me at any moment but it will only be granted when you are moving forward wholeheartedly in integrity with the strength of your will coinciding with the strength of divine will. For although they are the same thing in a certain way that you are divine creatures. The divine blueprint for humanity is set and fixed in the way that you must act in order to bring in the love for all humanity to fulfill your missions. Therefore go from the understanding of love that you already have to fusing with the divine light and the divine love of God and your laser focus will move you to the higher point of intelligence and the vessel that you are inhabiting will gel with your four body system and every step you make will be blessed. You will be a walking meditation, you will be a walking light, you will embody love and you will feel the power of this. Recognize that you are the power. Merge, synchronize, appreciate yourself for who you are and come home to your Power.

Your Merkaba has many different uses. Firstly it is the gateway to your higher consciousness, it is the Jacob's ladder, it is the Chariot with which you ascend and become one with everything. When you ascend initially you experience the oneness of all creation and this is a wonderful point in your changing evolution. Once you have done this it is only the beginning step in you reaching higher and higher levels of awareness and being able to move through the different dimensions, sitting in the steering point of your third eye within your vessel, within your consciousness. As you open up, as you learn to drive, as you move yourself forward in the different dimensions and experience the different frequencies of light and the different points of bliss you will be intoxicated and you will completely drop any thoughts of the pleasures that you used to get from the lower chakras for your awareness will be expanded. It is like having always lived in one room in a house and having never been outside but having enjoyed the different pleasures that are in this room and then walking outside and realising that there are mountains, rivers, beaches and that you can fly and swim and taste the nectar of divine light. Walk out of your little room and expand your awareness, come into your mastery.

Another use of the Merkaba is to go back in time in your consciousness. In your three-dimensional linear plane and see all the wonderful things and answer all the questions that you have about the past on your Earth plane. To stand as Jesus preached, to watch as Leonardo painted, to stand in awe as Mozart composed and played. This is part of what you can do with your Merkaba and this is a wonderful thing for when you understand that time can stand still and you can roam and explore the universe and your time lines and come back to exactly the same second you left your meditation you will be freed and your vessel will be rejuvenated. You will go into a state, the breathless state, the state of Samadhi where your body will not age and you will roam in your consciousness and this is a wonderful experience. Sitting with your consciousness in the place of your third eye you will become the witness to everything and you will be able to help all mankind steer themselves in the right direction.

There are many different dimensions and within this dimension there are many different timelines for you have free will and there are many different timelines that are happening simultaneously, different dimensions of the same existence. Within this linear timeline that you are leading you can move forward and explore the different choices that can be made by humanity, the choice to keep polluting your Earth plane, to keep polluting your selves.

The Earth will survive; it survived for millions and billions of years before you were here and will survive if you have to leave. We do not wish this for you, this is your home but you must start to be responsible if you are to stay here.

As Masters moving forward, being able to explore the different timelines within your Merkaba you will be able to see and help steer mankind in the right direction, by showing example, always creative, never competitive. For this is the truth of spirit, this is the truth of your co-creation, the truth of your interdependence, of you expanding your light and walking into your mastery and we are excited that you are coming to this point.

While sitting with your consciousness in your third eye hold the mudra of your thumb and your middle finger. Feel a ball of light between your hands. As you are holding this mudra feel yourself being able to steer left and right much like in your Car, your vehicles on the road, this will be left and right.

Also, when you pull back you will pull yourself up and when you push down you will go down as in your Aeroplanes.

Now imagine your timeline as a linear line and picture the date that you want to go back to or the event that you want to go back to. You have to feel this and picture this and imagine this and feel the special awareness of being in your third eye place.

You may manoeuvre around the place you have taken yourself to. The building of the Pyramids, Stonehenge, Atlantis, Lemuria, to the Native Americans when Christopher Columbus came to their shores or as the Conquistadors came to South America, as the Aborigines were seeded at Uluru, as Ankor Watt was built, as Krishna manifested, at the birth of Christ. All these places you can go and experience first hand, this is your wonderful rich history, which is to be honoured and appreciated.

Steer your Merkaba wherever you wish and enjoy yourself going backward in your linear time and moving forwards to the different possible futures you have for yourself but understand that if even if you roam for what seems like years when you come back you will come back to the same point within your linear time scale, for you all have a mission and it is within this linear time frame that you must achieve this mission.

Another use for your Merkaba is manifestation within the material plane. You can manifest money, you can manifest things, you can manifest dwelling places, and you can manifest help for others.

This is a powerful tool.

Once you truly pass the ring pass not you will not abuse this tool. You will have no wish to abuse this tool. But in understanding that you are the riches of the Universe you will not crave the same things that you crave when you are gripped by the lower chakras for you will understand that you are supported by all and you can create all and manifest whatever you desire and be at one with your consciousness. This is how the loaves and the fish were multiplied, this was an actual event, not just a metaphor in your bible and this is how it was achieved.

Thanks have to always be given, in other words you have to be in a frame of mind of gratitude that there is a continuum of wonderful abundance and your Merkaba will manifest all that you desire and all that you wish to help others.

68

This is a powerful tool, the most powerful tool that you can ever have. Respect this understanding and you will be taken to higher heights.

You can also heal with the Merkaba, you can heal any ailment within your own vessel and you can heal others, heal them fully and completely. This has to be in co-operation with his or her journey for everyone is on a spiritual path and the initial thought of the light worker is just to heal everyone. But that would defeat the purpose of going through the experience of creation. You must allow humanity to be allowed to experience their pain, to experience their struggles, their illness and feeling a lack of abundance for that is part of the whole point of creation that we may experience and then we may rise above. So although you may heal this has to be in accordance with people's free will and if they are willing and asking to be healed there is nothing that goes against the power of Grace. You will understand this more and more and you will instinctively know when someone is at the right point to be healed and is giving themselves over to the experience of reaching to the higher understanding of spirituality and their own selves and the fact that they can heal completely, unequivocally and totally.

Your Merkaba can also be used for bi-location, as multi dimensional beings this is a great use for your merkaba for in moving forward and in raising to the higher point of your consciousness people will look to you more and more and will see you as you move forward as a Godman/woman, as a deity. Part of your Adept-ship is to allow this if you are ready to take on the mantle of being worshipped. This is mostly for civilisations and cultures that are not ready to walk into their own mastery but it will mean that you are surrounded by people at all times. You do not have to take on this mantle as a Master. You can be in anonymity and this is where the bi-location brings in its great power for you can be with people without them seeing you and you can be with people while they are in danger and help them and as your consciousness expands and you are in different places simultaneously you will move forward towards your omnipresent energy. Your individualised vessel, although having a personality, through bi-location, which does include a sense of humour (Laughs) you may choose either way to do this. You may manifest yourself among the undiscovered tribes and there are still people on your Earth plane that have not been introduced to civilisation yet, these are the people who will look to you as a God and it is up to your discernment to lead them in the right direction. This is the power you are being given when you walk into the power of your merkaba. You may sit constantly in the Galactic Council when you learn to bi-locate properly. This will come with practice of using your merkaba and you will be asked for your opinion on matters that concern the wider Universe, the different Galaxies, the different dimensions, you will be given a vote and your vote will count for you would not be included within the Galactic Council if you were not ready to be heard and to have a valid, evolved point of view.

Your Merkaba affords you complete protection in the physical also in your three dimensional world. Within your physical vessel you need never worry about violence when you emancipate yourself fully unless you give yourself over to this as an example to help as Jesus did, as many God-men have done in the past. But this was his will in order to help humanity. To look to a higher ideal and to not be in violence, to be in truth, in love - and you will not be doing wrong by going through Jesus' name. He has been at the highest point of sacrifice in your linear time in humanity. But he did not have to do this for his Merkaba was fully opened. Understand that when you open your Merkaba fully you can be in the middle of a War zone with bombs exploding all around you and people firing grenades and machine guns and you will be completely protected. This will only be after you have passed the point of the ring pass not therefore it is important that you practice this and you do not fool yourself that you have moved past this point before you are ready.

The Merkaba will be used for many things and we have not stated all the things that your merkaba will be used for, you can also create Universes, be at the power to make creation and watch as it flowers and evolves. You must first practice the meditations we have given you. These are the beginning point of you becoming the Warriors that will transform your World.

Awaken to the truth of these statements and practice, practice, practice.

Fear must be taken out of the equation, for fear is of the duality and when you open up your merkaba properly you will become at one with the universe. Becoming at one with the universe takes away all duality and although you will still live in a material world on the Earth plane you will experience what it is to be enlightened and in this understanding fear will be taken out of the equation. This is why you have to battle the devil; this is why you have to bring yourself to the metaphor of transformation, overcoming Satan, overcoming your lower chakras and the fear that comes with that. You are mighty beings, this is you preparing yourself ready for the missions that you have ahead. The main mission that you will all have is to work on yourself and keep constant, be impeccable within yourselves and be on guard for your lower chakras creeping up for it is easy to get lazy and to understand that your negativity is there waiting to pounce therefore purify. When you move past the point of the ring pass not things will become much easier, fear will be taken out of the equation. Strive for this point, strive for this purity, open your hearts, be pure of heart for this is the truth of it being said blessed are the pure of heart for they will see god for when you open up your merkaba fully you will understand your true nature and you will see God, you will feel the love of the Father. It will encompass you, you will become one with it and this will bring you forward to a much higher place of vibration. Be brave be ready, your path is being laid before you, you must follow your bliss, of course you will help many others but you will help many others by spreading your own light, by being your own council and having the council of the Angels and the heavenly hierarchy.

This is important for opinion will take your from your path, frailty, or the belief in frailty will take you from your path, strive always for truth. Opinions are from peoples filter system but when their filter system is conquered, when it is cleared and when it is dealt with they begin to see the truth of their own selves. Truth is constant, truth is never changing, truth is never ending and the truth if the Universe is love, for God is Love, your essence is love. Therefore understand that this is not about your small self, having opinions of suspicion, this is about opening up to your warrior spirit and being brave enough to love, being brave enough not to fight, being brave enough to accept that the only fight in your life will be against yourself and conquering the negative energies that try to invade your consciousness. Be gentle as the lamb, you are being sent out amongst wolves but do not worry for the core of the Wolf is also love therefore transcend the duality and you will move yourself forward. Transcend the duality and focus upon your mission. The first step in this mission is opening up your merkaba. This call, to all light workers, to all who are feeling the transformation on the Earth plane at the moment, to all who feel that they have a higher purpose, who feel that there is something more, that they are not there, that they are not following the path that they are meant to be on – this is the first step. No matter what you are doing as a job right now, no matter the circumstances within your relationship right now, no matter the circumstances within your family or within your cultural experience, or within your personal physical vessel or within your country. The first step is to open up yourself, it begins with you and this is where your abundance will come in for having an abundance of spirit will translate to being an abundance in the material world and you will be able to spread that abundance. This is not just talking about money; this is talking about goodwill, a good attitude and turning things around for the ones that are not quite ready to be at the point where they are ready to open up their merkaba but they will feel the love and they will be inspired by you. By your reverence for life, by your joy, by your peace, by your stillness, by your laughter and by your fun, it will be contagious; you will be contagious in your joy, in your truth. Open up that light for this is your mission.

You must constantly push the boundaries of your capabilities for you are capable of much greatness - you are capable of much. Your transformation will be swift when you completely let go of fear, when you completely know what it is to open up your merkaba you will be bathed in divine light and your powerful energy will move forward a hundred fold. It will seem within the twinkling of an eye, which is where this saying comes from for enlightenment, oneness, becoming the oneness instead of the duality happens in the twinkling of an eye. It happens when you are ready for it and make yourself ready for it. Therefore do the merkaba meditation, believe in yourself, and believe in humanity. Believe in all those souls who seem to be lost but are only just learning how to become proper human beings and understand how to treat each other. Yes the World is in a state of chaos but there is a divine plan underneath this you must understand, respect and believe this divine plan in order to move yourself forward and become part of the divine plan, that you may do your part.

The old ways of preaching are gone; the preachers have to be your individual vessels, to yourselves. No longer is there a valid hierarchy on the Earth plane for each and every person will be your own priest, will be your own minister, will give your own spiritual lessons coming from the core of you which is all the same for you are all beings of love. Embody this truth and understand that you are moving towards a much better tomorrow. Everyone on the Earth plane can be fed, everyone on the Earth plane can be considered, everyone on the Earth plane can be enlightened and this is where you are moving. Embrace this time, embrace the conflict, embrace the contrast that you are being given on the Earth plane, embrace the understanding of war, embrace the understanding of the dark and the light, assimilate this completely within yourself and you will love everything for you will not be involved in the drama of it and you will be able to do some good in order to transform everybody from their understanding of what is in front of their faces to what is inside them and what can be and their co-creative powers and them moving forward to a much better tomorrow which is where you are moving towards therefore do not be in fear. Do not allow yourself to be in fear. Walk forward, you are mighty warriors, this is the time, this is the moment and your emancipation is at hand, the emancipation of the World is at hand. It will happen in the twinkling of an eye on an individual basis. There are many who are expecting a rapture of souls transforming and people on the Earth plane being judged and being killed and being slaughtered by the almighty. This is a man made concept; this is not the concept from the divine for the divine does not judge and you are being led into your divine selves therefore do not judge, judging is of the lower chakras, it is of the un-evolved self. You are not here to judge, you are here to evolve.

The reality that has been seen by the seers of the apocalypse is already happening with your wars, with your famine, with your greed and corruption. There is enough happening that is dreadful on the Earth plane that is as bad as any of your books of prophecy, as bad as the book of revelation, as bad as your soothsayers doom bringing prophesies. Understand that you are here to bring in the light, to bring in the love and to enlighten humanity to a better tomorrow. Not to contribute to the pain and the suffering. You are here to rise above it and the only way to rise above it is to not be in judgement, to not be in fear, to not worry about anything, move yourselves forward, follow your bliss.

As a divine spiritual warrior of the heavenly hierarchy you must chase whatever it is that gives you joy, that gives you bliss. Whether it be singing, dancing, acting, being a civil servant or a marine biologist, businessman, tycoon or being in the Red Cross helping people, everything is worthy when it is approached with passion, joy and love. With desire of the highest and utmost reverence for life and this is where you may live the best life you can live it does not matter your profession. But your profession matters - that you are following your path of bliss. This is important and this is what you are charged with – follow your bliss. Follow your desire, follow what it is that you would really love to do and be the best at it that you can be and this will be through meditation, through prayer, through purifying yourself and becoming the best that you can be through exercise, eating the right things, drinking pure water, lots of it. Mission has many faces and each and every profession is worthy at it's own level. If you are a light worker and you are a Butcher be the best butcher that you can be but as you raise your vibration you will not be able to handle working with dead animals anymore and you will move forward. If you are a soldier be the best soldier that you can be but you will not be able to handle the fact that you can be ordered to kill any more. If you are in crime, be the best criminal that you can be but you will not be able to be in this for very long for this is a hypocrisy against your true self and ALL are moving forward and are creating a different paradigm for themselves and this will be a much better tomorrow. So open yourselves up, honour where you are at the moment and evolve. Open yourself up and do not think your self better than anyone else for you are no better than anyone else but you are just as good and your potential can move you forward to a higher ideal of your self and your abundance will come in when you are on your true path for when you are in hypocrisy, leading the life that is incongruent with your spirit your abundance will not move forward. And this is abundance mentally, emotionally, physically and spiritually that you may be in joy, in peace, that you may have the peace that passes understanding and you may be contributing to a more enlightened world and you will move forward into the age of enlightenment, the Golden age.

Do not think your self unworthy but as you move into your centre, as you evolve and transform you will truly walk into your power and you will love being alive and all thoughts of negativity, of depression, of being unworthy and feeling hard done to, all the poor me energies will disappear for you will understand that you have an amount of time on this Earth plane, in this incarnation that you are to be in joy, fun, laughter and love and to further yourself and mankind. As you give to others you will give to yourself and you will come into alignment with your divine self and be able to walk the path without fear, without judgement, without negativity. This is a wonderful thing and we are with you no matter what you are doing right now you are not being judged. No matter what you are doing right now this will not bring you to negativity if you take upon the mantle of your true self. If you continue where you are if you are in a place that is incongruent with your spirit you will bring upon yourself more karma and pain and suffering but as you are reading this you are in a place of transformation. No matter what you have done in the past, you can purify, you can transform and you can open yourself up to this transformation and your aura, your merkaba and your chakras, your divine light will shine force and the effulgence of your true self will become apparent to all, they will see your light.

Open yourself up to your true self for now is the time, now is the call, now is the pull towards where you want to be. You want the suffering to end within yourself and within others, within the whole of mankind and move towards the Utopia that we can achieve together for all angels are working on the Earth plane with each and every one of you. We are ready, all you need to do is call upon us, do not be in hypocrisy any more. Even if you are seen as a pious person but you know you are in hypocrisy in your spirit do not worry, you can change, you can transform, this is part of your divine blueprint, open it up, do yourself a favour, transform, come into your enlightenment, this is the moment. We love you and are helping each and every one of you, we are opening up the gateway, the gateway is above your head, ready for you to transform your energies, plug yourselves into the Matrix of creation and become one with your creator, become one with the divine light that you are. Shake away the illusion and open up to the reality, the truth of love, the truth of your spirit, the power of your divine self and understand the frailty of the darkness on the Earth plane, the weakness that holds on, that tries to drain, that moves forward in psychic Vampirism, engendering suffering and the pulling of energy from others through fear, manipulation, corruption, negativity, rape, murder, extortion, all the negatives on your earth plane and even the subtle negatives within relationships. The subtle power plays of the tyrant Invalid who rules through a veneer of seeming weakness but with power brought in from pulling the energies from others through their compassion, bleeding and leaching. This transformation can be complete with all no matter what your physical circumstances understand there can be no 'poor me' anymore. Walk into your power, concentrate on what you can do not what you cannot do. Compassion is important for the light worker but not to the detriment of yourself and if you are being drained by someone who is acting as a Tyrant, you can break yourself free from this. The heavenly hierarchy are here to bring in the swords of discernment and cut the cords from the negatives and the Tyrant who is pulling the energy from you can be given more love, but it will be given with your discernment and your understanding of what they are doing. Do not be fooled, all are here contributing to this illusion at different stages of their evolution. Understand your own stage and walk into your Mastery

that no one may hold onto your energy strands apart from the ones that you give to freely. There will be no more draining of your energy when you fully spark open your merkaba and you will do them more good, you will benefit them more freely, fully and wholeheartedly and they will be inspired to a higher ideal.

This does not take a sacrifice; the only sacrifice you have to give is to let go of your lower self and move forward to your higher self and in walking forward as a master, what may seem as being a sacrifice from you as you giving yourself will not be a sacrifice for it will be in love, it will be in truth, in power and strength, the strength of the Master. Become that divine master; these things all the divine masters of the past have done before you too can do. All the materialisation, all the healing, the bi-location, manifestation, the bringing in of abundance, open up your divine light for the kingdom of god is within you, you access this through your merkaba, through the divine light, through your chosen deity or my name. The name is not as important as the understanding that love is all, therefore bathe your self in love. Love in the morning, love in the afternoon, go to bed at night with love. You will transform your life completely and you will be worthy to move through the ring pass not and your mastery will be complete and you will teach through your actions. We urge you forward and push you forward toward your destiny, your design. Time is of the essence; it is now time to get excited about your mission, of understanding your power and the glory of the Father that is being born in and through you. You are an experience of god in evolution. God is experiencing life through you, understand your divinity, understand your divine nature, become at one and look through the eyes of purity, of love, of truth, of divine sacrifice, of understanding what you have to do, what your bliss is pulling you forward to.

We love you, we *are* you, we rejoice in you reading these words and you assimilating this truth within yourself. Test this, we do not ask for blind faith, test this, test the divine love and come closer. As you move one step towards us we move a hundred towards you. As you make the first step towards God we open a thousand doors for you to walk through, for you to choose and when you are walking forward in your integrity, with purity, you cannot make a mistake in walking forward for your light will be shone wherever it is needed. Your influence will be felt and you will inspire others towards their divine selves. Therefore practice the meditations, practice walking forward in purity, practice being out of your hypocrisy and into your divinity. Practice the oneness of life and you will contribute greatly to where humanity is heading and your life will transform into a symphony of beautiful music, into rays of divine light of all the colours of the spectrum, Into the light that is your birth right, into the life that you could only ever before imagine. Trust yourself, trust your core, trust us, dive deeply into the ocean of awareness and immerse yourself in love. This is your mission.

The heavenly hierarchy rejoices in you reaching this point in your evolution. For you are moving past the point of conflict, the point of duality, the point of negativity and understanding that you are creating the illusion that you are seeing which is a wonderful thing for in understanding the power of your creative abilities you will create the new Heaven on Earth. This is the understanding of your consciousness for the afterlife as far as your understanding has been of a duality of an understanding that Heaven is a place that you go to be rewarded and Hell is a place you go to be punished. You must come to the understanding of your own divinity and transcend this duality in negativity and simplistic understanding. The Hell of your punishment is of your own consciousness and Hell is very real when you are immersed in your lower chakras, when you are allowing your vessel to take control and feed into the duality of your creation you can create a Hell on Earth and when you transcend without your physical body before you are re-incarnated you can understand within your consciousness the experience of being in a place of purgatory, Before you are re-incarnated and have another chance to ascend, to evolve, to transform your consciousness. But this is only a point of consciousness. The real understanding of Heaven is an understanding of who you really are of your own divinity. It is not a place of reward; it is a place of transcendence, of oneness, of purity, of light, of power. Of understanding where you were in the beginning before you went on this journey of creation, of consciousness, becoming one with the Father.

You are mighty beings, you are creator beings and this is the point where you are getting ready to embody your power. So take it upon yourself, move this forward and take it upon yourself to transcend your consciousness. This is an exciting time and you are ready, you are ready to create, ready to be in joy, ready to be in bliss and you are ready to embody your power. So open up to this truth, become the divine oneness that is your divine birthright. You were always being led to this point. Open up to the Angels, open up to your guides, open up to the deities, open up to the truth of the oneness that is you. Let go of negativity and embody the joy of your creation.

We will be with you every step of the way and we are always here waiting for your call, waiting for you to move yourselves to this higher point of consciousness, to bathe in the divine light. Each and every one of you on the Earth plane is transforming and changing but the light workers that have got to this point in the book are ready. This will require practice, this will require steadfastness, this will require you sacrificing your lower self for a higher understanding, a higher truth, a higher peace, a higher love - Unconditional.

You are ready, take the steps that we have outlined in this book and you will move yourselves forward and become at one with everything and become the masters that you are here to become. Your missions will accelerate, your personal power will become immense and you will no longer be in pain, no longer be in suffering, no longer allow the negativity of anyone who wishes to keep you in the duality to hold you down or your own vessel, your own chakras. You are creating the new Heaven and Earth, you are the future in your linear time scale on this plane of consciousness.

Be brave, be in Joy, and be at Peace.

I am Archangel Metatron, I am with you always and I love you, each and every one of you.

Do not be afraid - be at Peace.

Made in the USA
Lexington, KY
09 July 2015